ABOUT THE AUTHOR

Nick Baker, author, 1992 Olympic Coach, and founder of Peak Performance Swim Camp is proud to introduce his sixth book, *Mind Body Skill*. His insights are the result of a professional coaching career spanning 46 years. Over that time, Coach Baker has worked with swimmers of all ages and abilities including world-record holders, Olympic finalists, and NCAA champions.

Before coaching, he swam for a total of ten years and qualified for the Olympic Trials in the 200-breaststroke. Altogether, he has spent 56 years in a sport he truly loves.

Coach Baker's top priority is to help swimmers achieve their peak potential through a holistic training approach which places an equal emphasis on mental, technical, and physical conditioning. His best-selling book, *The Swimming Triangle*, outlines this approach in great depth and detail.

In addition to training swimmers in the United States, Coach Baker travels the world. Over the past 25 years, he has conducted 500 plus swim camps and clinics in more than 20 different countries.

Peak Performance Swim Camp is a proud partner of NIKE/US Sports Camps. For information visit *www.swimcamp.com* or call 877.308.PEAK (7325). You can also find us on Facebook, Twitter, and Instagram @swimcamp

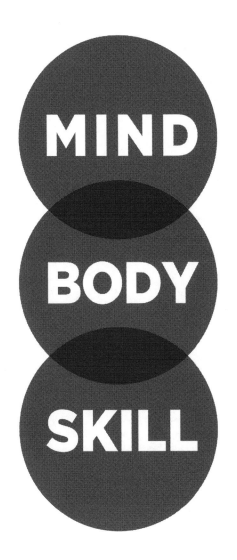

BALANCE IN THE SPORT OF SWIMMING ISN'T SOMETHING YOU FIND, IT'S SOMETHING YOU CREATE ON A DAILY BASIS.

— COACH NICK BAKER

TABLE OF CONTENTS

TABLE OF CONTENTS (CONTINUED)

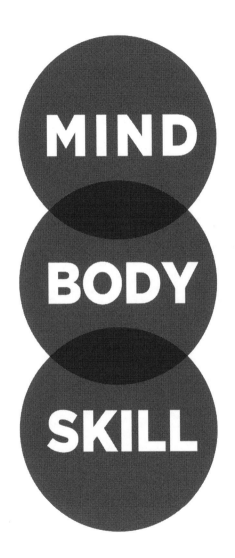

MIND BODY SKILL INTRODUCTION

Choosing the subtitle for my newest book was a challenge because I wanted to convey the right message. After much thought, I decided on "A Journey To Swimming Excellence" because the word "journey" depicts the act of traveling from one place to another. Your journey began when you joined your local swim team, and it will continue as long as you have a passion for swimming. In the beginning, you probably struggled (as most do), but now you have things under control to one degree or another. Your current level of expertise is the result of your natural ability, your effort thus far, and the quality of coaching you've received up to this point in your career. While your coach oversees your journey and ensures that you receive the ideal mix of teaching, training, and competing; you also have a significant role to play in your development, part of which involves seeking alternative ways (outside of your daily swimming routine) to boost your performance. My role (as the book's author) is that of an assistant coach here to guide and advise you on how best to advance your mind, body, and skill to a level of swimming excellence. If you're like most swimmers, your journey will span a decade or more, and in that time you'll experience many ups and downs. But take heart, because with the right steps you'll be victorious. If you're relatively new to the sport of swimming, I advise you to walk first, jog second, and run third. In other words, seek small improvements at the beginning and grow from there. Over time, your victories will create an insatiable appetite to do more and to become better. This "walk-jog-run approach" isn't new or revolutionary as every successful swimmer begins their journey walking.

MIND

Your mind is your greatest asset of all as it holds the key to unlocking your swimming future. Think of it as an internal compass, designed to point you in the direction of your dreams. It controls every thought you think, every action you take, and every result you achieve in swimming (and in life). If you keep your mind in step with your journey, you'll be successful, and if not, there's no telling where you'll end up. That's why it's vitally important to continually feed your mind "success nutrients" like positivity, determination, and patience, so that it can function at its best and deliver the results that you crave.

BODY

While your mind provides the THINKING part of your swimming, your body supplies the DOING part. For example, the mind maps out the action of the butterfly, but your body must work to make it happen. The best way to condition your body is through a combination of pool-based training and dry-land training that enhances your endurance, strength, and flexibility to the fullest.

From an endurance standpoint, pool-based training is the primary way to boost swimming stamina, while alternative activities like running, trampolining, rowing, cycling, and even boxing can add additional benefits. It's worth noting that every racing distance in swimming (including the 50) has an endurance requirement, so even sprint-orientated swimmers need to focus on it in training.

From a strength standpoint, swim-specific drills (like pulling against resistance and vertical kicking), are ideal strength builders combined with various forms of dry-land training like calisthenics, plyometrics, gymnastics, medicine balls, weights, and Pilates. Creating a surplus of strength will allow your body to operate at peak levels. I think of strength as the "secret sauce" that makes everything in swimming that much better.

From a flexibility standpoint, yoga and stroke-specific stretches are excellent options for increasing your range of motion and adding power to your starts, strokes, and turns. You may wonder how flexibility enhances power so allow me to give you a simple example. A swimmer who can swing their arms beyond shoulder height on a Throw & Go Front Start will generate far more starting power off the block compared to a swimmer who can only swing them halfway there. Improvements in flexibility will also help to relax your body allowing you to move through the water with greater ease.

The ideal amount of endurance, strength, and flexibility training performed per week in practice is dependent upon your age, your current level of performance, and your long-term swimming objectives. Additional information regarding age-specific training is available in my second book *The Swimming Triangle*.

SKILL

Developing the skills needed to excel in the demanding world of competitive swimming is not rocket science, but rather a time-honored tradition that should begin early on in your swimming journey. Step one involves learning the various skills that constitute a particular start, stroke, turn, or finish. Step two consists of perfecting these skills in practice to the point where they become part of you. Step three is the tricky one as it involves performing them successfully in competition. The phrase "automate to be great" underlies the importance of learning the correct skills early on to excel further down the road. A few years back I conducted a swim camp in Barcelona, one week before the World Swimming Championships. PEAK shared the pool with Olympic swimmers from Japan and the Netherlands. Each day I watched in awe as these amazing swimmers trained with flawless technique, and it was no surprise to me when I watched them compete (one week later) in the very same manner.

MISSION IMPOSSIBLE

No one likes to hear bad news, but I have some to share. Unless you can keep your "swimming vibe" alive, you'll run out of gas well before the finish line! That's because swimming can be tough, tedious, and unrewarding (at times) leaving you feeling drained and lifeless. To thrive and survive in this demanding environment you must become the "driver of your dream" and push on no matter what the circumstances! But that's not enough on its own. You must also exercise a high degree of maturity, take responsibility for your actions, and be able to withstand the impulse to quit when things don't go your way. Without you in the driver's seat, swimming excellence is nothing more than a wish!

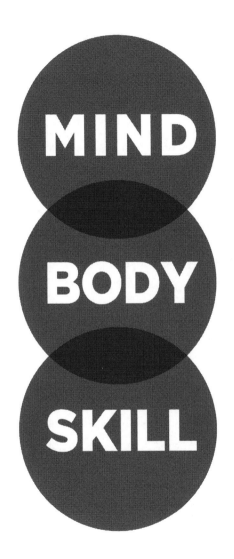

MIND WORK

INTRODUCTION

When I was a kid in the 1950s, I loved to play with magnets and thought they were really cool. When I placed the North Pole end of one magnet against the South Pole end of another, they'd attract each other, but when I put like poles together (North to North or South to South), they'd repel each other. At this point, you're probably wondering, what magnets have to do with the mind and swimming fast? Strangely enough, there is a correlation as positive thoughts attract success like opposite ends of two magnets, while negative thoughts repel it. To advance your swimming journey and ensure victory, you must be actively engaged in creating a success mindset from dawn to dusk.

LEAD WITH YOUR BRAIN

Do you have a well-functioning brain? If so, it's time to put it in control of your swimming journey much like a TV remote controls a TV. Use it to focus on learning, and it will make you a more skillful swimmer. Use it to push yourself, and it will make you a harder worker. And use it to visualize a winning performance, and it will make you a swimming champion. Your body is ready for action, but it needs your brain to take the lead.

SUIT OF ARMOR

Back in the medieval times, knights wore suits of armor to protect themselves in battle. Their armor was made of steel and shielded them from arrows, swords, and spears. Olympic swimmers are protected by armor as well, but not the steel kind of course because they'd sink! Theirs consists of mental toughness, a quality forged through years of extreme hardship. The chances are that when you watch the Olympians compete, you think how lucky they are and how easy they have it. In reality, it hasn't been easy for them, and that's why they're so successful. To achieve Olympic status, you must be able to endure the toughest of times year-after-year. Take Michael Phelps for example. Over his star-studded career, he won 23 Olympic gold medals, and every time he stood on the block, he was expected to win. Not only win but break the world record in the process! It didn't matter how he felt mentally or physically on any given day, he faced the world's best and won time-after-time. Imagine if you were in his shoes? Could you have handled it? You could if you had your own suit of armor. The next time you find yourself going through a difficult time, thank your lucky stars because it's preparing you for greatness!

CLARITY OF PURPOSE

Although the truth may hurt, swimmers aren't always the deepest of thinkers. I've encountered many who honestly believe that if they just show up to practice, they'll make the Olympic team one day! I'm not sure if it's a lack of insight, lazy-brain syndrome, wishful thinking, or reality avoidance, but regardless of the reason, it's definitely not happening for them. Those who reach the pinnacle of success have clarity of purpose (a clear understanding) of what they need to do to make their swimming dreams come true. Allow me to give you a light-hearted example of how a lack of clarity can have adverse effects. Let's pretend that you're absolutely starving, so you go off to the grocery store, wander aimlessly up and down the aisles filling up your shopping cart. You return home with a bag full of light bulbs, dish soap, masking tape, cat litter, magazines, aluminum foil, lottery tickets, and toilet paper! Now, allow me to give you a second example of how clarity can have favorable effects. Let's pretend that you're absolutely starving, so you sit down and make a detailed list of the foods you crave. From there, you go off to the grocery store and fill up your shopping cart with the items on your list. You return home with a bag full of apples, bananas, blueberries, yogurt, milk, peanut butter, bagels, cream cheese, salad fixings, chicken, pasta, and chocolate chip ice cream. In the first scenario, you lacked clarity of purpose while in the second it was loud and clear. Knowing why you swim and staying true to the "why" is the only way to navigate your journey successfully.

COMBAT SPORT

From the outside looking in, swimming can appear to be a gentler sport when compared to football, lacrosse, or hockey; but in reality, it can be just as rough and tumble. Not in the physical sense, but in a mental one. It can start with a lousy swim meet performance followed by the negative fallout that often ensues, like demeaning comments made by people in your inner circle. And it doesn't necessarily stop there. Your coach can ignore you or you can be teased by your fellow teammates, causing you to crash and burn emotionally. To excel in the pool, you must protect yourself from the "hits", in the same way that helmets and pads protect football players. While there's no type of physical protection that you can wear to blunt the mental blows, there are ways to shield yourself. Examples include not internalizing the negative words of others, seeing the good in bad situations, and using positive affirmations to combat the unfortunate daily onslaught of negativity that we all experience in life. As a coach, I wish that every swimmer (regardless of their ability) received the support and empathy they need and deserve so that they could fully blossom, but at least for now, the world doesn't work that way.

BREAKING POINT

The ability to push the mind to its breaking point is critical in a sport where there are no boundaries. Sadly, most swimmers lack the guts for it and back off when the pain becomes too intense. The problem with this approach is that it interferes with their progress because they never get past their current "pain point." One of the biggest challenges you'll ever face in swimming is dealing with the mental and physical anguish associated with high-performance training and competing, and the only way to overcome it is to meet the anguish head-on. Try putting your head down and go five more strokes or five more seconds before giving in. In time, your tolerance for pain will grow bigger and bigger, and you'll get better and better.

PAY YOUR DUES

I love watching motivational videos. One of my favorites is *Mind Shift*. In the video, motivational guru Tony Robbins states, "People are rewarded in public for what they've been doing for years in private." In other words, they paid their dues over time and are now reaping the rewards. Wouldn't life be a breeze if you could snap your fingers and have whatever you wanted without paying your dues first? Sadly, it doesn't work that way. Swimming excellence is a marathon and not a sprint. So if you want it all, put in the work and wait for the rewards to come.

DON'T THINK, ACT

Achieving excellence in swimming is all about taking action. Stepping up to the challenge at hand is a success ingredient common to all Olympic swimmers. Their immediate response is to go for it, no matter what IT is. They don't spend time pondering the possibilities because they know that success waits for no man or woman. An instant response also eliminates restrictive thinking like "What if I can't?" or "What if I fail?" Thoughts like these are "excellence killers" because they freeze you in place and prevent you from taking the necessary steps needed to excel.

SMILE OFTEN

The act of smiling releases neuropeptides (nerve proteins) that regulate the way that cells communicate with each other. Neuropeptides influence the brain, body, and behavior in many ways, including energy levels, learning, memory, sleep, and stress. Through smiling, the brain releases feel-good neurotransmitters, including dopamine, endorphins, and serotonin. Dopamine gives the brain energy, motivation, and is necessary for habit change. Endorphins reduce the perception of pain and trigger a positive euphoric feeling in the body. Serotonin is considered the confidence molecule and increases feelings of well-being and self-worth. These brain chemicals also aid in calming the nervous system by lowering the heart rate and blood pressure. To harness the power of your smile and boost your brain, body, and swimming, take one-minute "smile breaks" throughout the day. It may sound weird and a strange thing to do, but next to sleep, it's probably the most enjoyable thing that you can do to enhance your swimming performance.

MAGNIFYING GLASS

If I were to ask you to list the characteristics common to Olympic swimmers you'd probably end up with a bad case of writer's cramp. No doubt you'd include a strong work ethic, tons of confidence, supreme fitness, near-perfect technique, mental toughness, calm under pressure, and high-self worth. While all of this (and more) is true, they also possess something that's unique. What's that? It's the ability to maintain an intense mental focus from the beginning of practice to the end. Their focus is like a giant magnifying glass that intensifies the positive benefits of training. If you tend to be a scatterbrain in practice, I have great news! There are numerous drills that you can employ to improve your focus ability. One of which involves closing your eyes and picking one thing to think about for a one-minute duration. It could be swimming related, your pet, favorite food, or best friend. It doesn't matter what it is as long as you can maintain it. If you lose focus, open your eyes, reset, and try again. Over time, expand the duration of your attention from one minute to two minutes and beyond. You can practice before going off to sleep at night or while traveling in the car, and the more often you do it, the stronger your "focus muscle" becomes. One word of caution, do not perform this drill in the car if you're the one driving it!

DEFINE YOURSELF

One of my favorite mental strategies is to have swimmers choose an animal that best defines their training attitude versus their racing attitude. An ideal example might be, pit bull in training and pit bull in racing, meaning high energy and tenacious. As you might expect, I've heard hundreds of combinations, and some have been quite strange. An 11-year-old swimmer named Emily picked her pet pussycat for her training attitude and a lion for her racing one! The moment she completed her sentence, alarm bells sounded in my head, and I quickly explained to her that pussycats don't survive in the swimming jungle. She smiled, paused for a moment, and said, "I get it, I need to be more aggressive in training." Precisely my point and from then on her times dropped like a rock!

GOALS ONLY WORK IF YOU DO

There was a time when I'd ask swimmers, "What is your ultimate swimming goal?", and most would respond with "To win an Olympic gold medal" or "To get a swimming scholarship." A few years back I rephrased the question and asked, "What swimming goal are you willing to work your butt off for?" I rephrased it because without work no meaningful goal is achievable! Let me repeat that sentence again, without work no meaningful goal is achievable! If a swimmer has the goal of making the Olympic team, they'd better be prepared for a decade or more of mind-numbing work and sacrifice, spending 24 hours or more a week training, and living the life of a hermit! Even then the odds are quite slim. In today's culture, few swimmers understand the degree of commitment and hard work needed to hit the big time in swimming. They live in tiny "swimming bubbles" and think that because they say they want something, it will magically materialize before their very eyes. Questioning your goal (from time-to-time) is a critical step in the success process, because unless you're all in (mind, body, skill), you're just wasting your precious time. Ask yourself, "Do I really want what I think I want and am I willing to sacrifice everything to achieve it?" If "yes," go for it, if "maybe" or "no," downsize your goal or pick something more realistic.

DON'T BE AFRAID

No two people think alike, sound alike, or look alike. Even identical twins aren't one hundred percent the same. The differences are not coincidental, but rather part of God's plan. Having the courage to follow one's destiny is one of life's most significant challenges. Whenever I meet and work with a swimmer for the very first time, I conduct a talent search, meaning I look for technical and physical evidence that indicates their level of natural swimming ability. I also engage them in a casual conversation to gather additional coaching intelligence. Ninety-nine percent of the time I conclude that they're swimming below their peak potential, and when I ask why, they usually tell me that they're afraid or fearful. How very sad! Perhaps you share their feelings, and if so, you're not alone. Regardless, you must never fear your potential, but rather embrace it and go full steam ahead. Fortunately, you don't have to do it all at once. Instead, be like a turtle and stick your neck out one practice and one race at a time.

A TEST OF GRIT

The standard swim team structure consists of levels and lanes, where swimmers are grouped based on their current level of swimming ability and performance. The benefits for those placed at (or near) the top are enormous as they feel far more appreciated and typically get special attention from the coach. On the flip side, swimmers assigned to lower levels and slower lanes can often feel underrated and disheartened. For them, this becomes a test of grit. Do they have the willpower and mental toughness to fight back and crawl to the top? If so, they'll be rewarded many times over, and if not, they'll stay at the bottom of the heap and fight for scraps. It may seem unfair, but competitive swimming is a "dog-eat-dog world" and those who can take it, make it! How about you? Do you have what it takes?

EXCUSE MACHINES

Over the years I've encountered many swimmers who were experts at making excuses. No matter what went wrong, they had a reason for it, and it was never their fault! They'd blame their coach, parents, and even the swimming pool, but it was never due to them. And to be honest, it's getting worse (in this day and age) as I encounter more and more "excuse machines" in my travels. Unfortunately, many swimmers are unwilling to accept the fact that their current state of swimming is due in large part to their own behavior, but rather than OWN IT, they live in denial and make up excuses. To avoid this performance pitfall, you'd be wise to take a reality check (from time-to-time) to ensure that you're swimming in the real world and not in a fantasy one. By reality check, I mean are you actually doing the things you need to do to achieve what you want in swimming?

FAILING WORDS

The usage of the word TRY drives me absolutely crazy and is overused by swimmers to the nth degree. I refer to it as a failing word because it creates a losing mindset. Over the years, I've had swimmers tell me that "they'll try to do this" or "they'll try to do that," yet put in a half-hearted effort and fail! The problem is that there are many shades of try, so that a swimmer can put forth an effort, but it's still not their very best or enough to succeed. Whenever I hear swimmers use the word try in a sentence like "I'll try to make the interval next time," I politely intervene and ask them to replace it with the word WILL. Although it may seem like a minor change, it's a far more powerful word that dramatically increases the likelihood of success.

Another failing word is HOPE, especially in a sport where success is the result of one's inner drive rather than some mysterious outside force (like aliens). Whenever I hear swimmers use the word hope in a sentence like "I hope to make finals today," I respond by saying, "Forget that, I've been hoping to win the lottery for fifty years and it hasn't happened yet!" Rather than rely on hope, they should rely on their God-given talent and hard work!

The final failing word is PROBABLY. If the weatherman told you that it was probably going to rain today, does that mean it will or won't? In the same way, if swimmers tell me that they probably need to do a better job in practice, does that mean they will or they won't?

Eliminating failing words from your swimming vocabulary and replacing them with productive words that deliver the results you seek is the only way to go!

SWIMMING IQ

The term IQ stands for intelligence quotient, a measurement of a person's intelligence expressed by a number. A person with a 100 IQ is considered smarter than the average person, while a genius has an IQ ranging from 120-140. Although IQ refers to matters of the brain, I believe there's another type that relates to a combination of a swimmer's mind and body. I call it "Swimming IQ" and define it as a measurement of a swimmer's mental capacity to learn high-performance swimming skills and their physical ability to perform them. For example, a swimmer with a high Swimming IQ for the butterfly will find the stroke easy to understand and swim, while a swimmer with a low Swimming IQ for the breaststroke will find it most difficult. All too often, swimmers give up on a stroke (hopefully not you) believing that they aren't meant to swim it, but that's definitely the wrong choice. If you find yourself lacking in a particular stroke, take heart! You can boost your Swimming IQ in a variety of ways including an improved focus in practice, targeted skill progressions, private lessons, specific strength and flexibility exercises geared to stroke weaknesses, and better coaching. Visualization techniques, where you envision yourself performing the stroke correctly (in your mind), are also very beneficial and highly recommended.

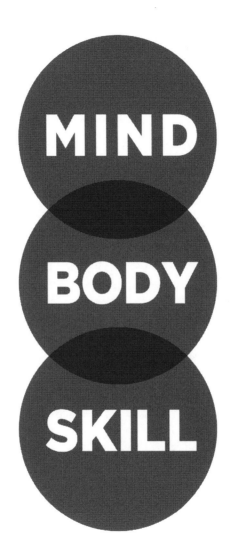

BODY WORK

INTRODUCTION

While a winning mindset is an essential part of your swimming journey, so too is a strong, flexible, and enduring body that functions at peak levels for the duration of any racing distance. I know many swimmers who can swim forever, but do so with short strokes due to a lack of strength. Others can power themselves down the pool (like a nuclear reactor), but fade after the first 50 due to a lack of endurance. On the contrary, Olympic swimmers have the whole package because they spend their training days enhancing their bodies in a three-sided fashion (endurance, strength, and flexibility). They do so because they're driven by an intense desire to succeed no matter what the cost, and recognize the importance of being physically well-rounded. To be truthful, you can be the most ambitious swimmer on the planet (with visions of Olympic medals dancing in your head), but unless your body can back it up, it won't happen in a million years!

ATHLETE FIRST

Occasionally, I like to play tricks on my swimmers to keep them on their toes. Recently I brought a group together and asked, "If you're a swimmer first, raise your hand." Of course, they took the bait and most raised their hands (except the veterans who know me best). I then asked, "If you're an athlete first, and a swimmer second, raise your hand." The ones who raised their hands the first time shouted, "That's not fair!" claiming now to be both an athlete and a swimmer. I happen to believe that there's a gigantic difference in the mindset between the two groups. An athlete first is willing to step outside their comfort zone and pursue other fitness activities to enhance their swimming, resulting in dynamic starts, strokes, and turns. On the flip side, those who see themselves as a swimmer first, tend to get all (or most) of their physical training through pool work alone. As a result, their start, stroke, and turning actions lack sparkle! So what group do you belong too? If you're a swimmer first, no worries because there's still time to turn your thinking and body around. You can start by incorporating a dry-land training routine into your daily schedule. If you're unsure where to start, I recommend purchasing my *PEAK OUT Dry-land Training Video* created by swim coach Kymmie Johnson. I promise that it will boost your swimming performance in a matter of weeks, and it's available online at swimcamp.com. If you already follow a fitness routine (outside of the water), try mixing it up by incorporating alternative exercises from other disciplines like Pilates for increased core strength, gymnastics for heightened body awareness and power, and dance for improved posture.

29 AND COUNTING

Once and for all I need to set the record straight. The core is much more than a six-pack and includes 29 different muscle groups! Many coaches tread lightly when discussing the role it plays in fast swimming because it's difficult for most swimmers to comprehend. Also, the terminology is somewhat tricky to pronounce compared to other forms of swimming jargon. To educate and motivate you, I've taken the liberty of highlighting the primary core muscle groups as well as examples of how they benefit your swimming.

The primary muscles of the core include:

- Rectus Abdominis
- External Obliques
- Internal Obliques
- Tranversus Abdominis

- Quadratus Lumborum
- Erector Spine
- Multifidus
- Semispinalis
- Latissimus Dorsi
- Iliopsoas
- Pelvic Floor
- Gluteus Maximus
- Gluteus Medius
- Gluteus Minimus

The benefits of a stronger core include:

- Helps to maintain a rigid streamlined body position in all starts, turns, and the breast-stroke-streamline position.
- Creates a rigid link between the arms and upper body and the legs and lower body that promotes a stronger pull and kick in all four strokes.
- Helps to prevent a side-to-side "fishtailing" action (of the body) in the backstroke and freestyle.
- Allows the arms and legs to act as propellors (rather than stabilizers) in the backstroke and freestyle.
- Helps to strengthen the chest-pressing action in the butterfly and the lunge-forward action in the breaststroke.
- Reduces drag by keeping the arms and legs closer to the surface when swimming the butterfly and breaststroke.
- Reduces drag by keeping the arms and legs closer to the body when pulling and kicking in the backstroke and freestyle.
- Helps to generate greater body roll in the backstroke and freestyle resulting in a stronger pull.

If you're unsure of what exercises strengthen a specific core muscle group, I suggest searching the internet. For example, if you're looking for exercises to enhance your Rectus Abdominis, search "Rectus Abdominis strength exercises."

MOVIE STAR

If climbing to the top of the film industry were an easy task, the world would have countless movie stars. The same odds exist if you thirst to make the Olympic Team one day. To have any chance at all, swimmers must be at the top of their game for multiple years. Not only that, but they must be willing, ready, and able to push their bodies to the breaking point day in and day out. To give you a better sense of the type of work you'll need to experience and endure, I researched Katie Ledecky's training history from age 10 to 15 (her age when she made the Olympics for the very first time).

Age 10
Practices: 5-6 per week
Distance Swum: 20-25 kilometers (roughly 12-15 miles)

Age 11-12
Practices: 6-7 per week
Distance Swum: 35-40 kilometers (roughly 21-24 miles)

Age 13-14
Practices: 7-8 per week
Distance Swum: 40-50 kilometers (roughly 24-31 miles)

Age 15
Practices: 9 per week

Distance Swum: 60-70 kilometers (roughly 37-42 miles)

HORIZONTAL JUMPS

Most swimmers are familiar with an exercise known as the vertical jump, designed to build leg strength for starts and turns. There's also another kind that swimmers do countless times in practice. It's known as the horizontal jump or pushing off the walls in a streamlined horizontal position. To advance this all-important turning skill, swimmers must contract their ankles, knees, and hips quickly and thoroughly each time they push off a wall. While leg strength plays a significant role in fast turns, complete and rapid muscle-contractions (of these three joint areas) adds additional speed and distance. To get your legs in blast-off shape give these two dry-land exercises a try:

Weight-Release Jump: Grab a pair of light dumbbells and hold them by your sides with your palms facing inward. Dip your knees (to the halfway point) and then explode upward as high as you can. As your feet leave the ground, release the dumbbells from your hands. Perform multiple sets of three to five repetitions, adding heavier weights in time.

Depth Jump: Stand on the edge of a 12-inch box or bench. Step off the box landing softly on the balls of your feet followed by your heels. Both of your feet should hit the ground at the same time. Upon contact, bend your knees again, and explode upwards as high as you can. Perform multiple sets of five to eight repetitions, increasing the number of sets in time.

BODY TYPES

Some swimmers have the perfect swimming body. They're long and lean and move through the water like a dolphin. They didn't get that way entirely on their own; they got some help from God. Others are "hybrids" meaning they possess a mixture of physical characteristics (some good and some bad).

The next time you're at a swim meet, take a good look at the swimmers standing on the blocks, then watch them race. What you'll soon discover is that it's almost impossible to predict the winner based on body type alone, and that's terrific news for the many! It's not uncommon to see a "twig" beat a super-muscular swimmer, a "vertically challenged" swimmer beat a taller one, or a chubby swimmer beat a skinny one. If you lucked out and your body looks similar to that of Michael Phelps, thank your lucky stars! If not, keep in mind that all swimmers (even Olympians) come in different shapes and sizes, so buckle down and focus on making your body the most fit it can get! On a side note, did you know that having too much muscle can increase drag and having too little body fat can decrease buoyancy?

T-I-E

For most swimmers, endurance training is a crucial part of every practice, but over time the benefits can diminish if performed with inferior technique or insufficient effort. To maximize the results, swimmers must focus on technical and physical intensity versus physical intensity alone. Endurance sets that lack these two essential ingredients are no more than "garbage-yardage sets" in disguise. To remind swimmers of this all-important concept, I created the acronym T-I-E which stands for technique, intensity, endurance.

MUSCLE TENSION

Many physical factors play a role in fast swimming, one of which includes muscle tension. If the amount is just right, swimmers will feel super-fast in the water, but if it's too low, they'll feel sluggish and slow. A lack of rest (before a major competition) may be the primary reason for a lackluster performance, but it could also be over-rested muscles that lack sufficient tension to fire fast and exert maximal force. You can prevent this from happening by keeping track of your muscle tension (weeks and days) before a competition. All you have to do is perform a short set of clap push-ups and vertical jumps (in succession for maximum height). If you feel super explosive, it means that your muscle tension is where it needs to be, and if not, it means that it's too low. Both tests are excellent first steps in letting you know how physically prepared you are to compete. If the results suggest that you lack sufficient muscle tension, you should increase the amount of sprinting in practice, add strength exercises to your daily training regime (push-ups, core work, and squats), and take ice baths (for the brave-hearted). You may want to try ice bath therapy during a time in the season when you're not approaching a significant competition to see how your body responds.

The chances are that you're familiar with how to perform a vertical jump, but you may not be as familiar with a clap push-up. To begin, assume a standard push-up position with your feet wider than hip-width apart. Next, drive the palms of your hands off the ground and perform a quick handclap before returning your palms to the ground. Be aware, that you'll need to have fast hands otherwise you could face-plant!

BMI

In competitive running, body type means everything. Sprint runners need lots of muscle, but all that bulk can be detrimental in longer-distance events. Competitive swimmers, on the other hand, are different than runners. In a recent scientific study published in Royal Study B (a British biological research journal) researchers measured the BMI (body mass index) of elite runners and swimmers to determine their percentage of body fat. To their surprise, they found that BMI scores dropped significantly in runners as event distances got longer, but not in the case of swimmers. Among female and male Olympians, BMI scores hovered around 21 and 23 respectively regardless of the racing distance. The study concluded that shorter, well-muscled, swimmers could compete effectively against taller and leaner ones if both shared a similar BMI, excellent news for those who believe that they can't compete due to their body shape or size. BMI scores of tested PEAK swimmers ranged from the high teens to the low twenties which is excellent news indeed. To determine your BMI, download a

BMI app on your computer or phone.

POSTURE

Swimmers are well known for their poor posture; the primary symptoms include thoracic spinal flexion, rounded shoulders, forward head position, flat lumbar spine, a forward-leaning of the hips, and a slight pelvic tilt. Enthusiasts will find this news disappointing as swimming is considered the best all-around sport from a health and conditioning standpoint. Perhaps so, but it does have some definite drawbacks. Specifically, it fails to develop the deep postural muscles of the hips and torso because swimmers aren't required to support their body weight against gravity (unlike athletes who stand). In time, this lack of gravitational pull on the body weakens the postural and stabilizing muscles. Poor land posture can affect swimmers in the water by increasing drag, reducing power, and lowering lung capacity (making it harder to breathe). It can also result in swimmer's shoulder, rotator cuff injuries, tendonitis, and overall degeneration.

Taking action beforehand is the best way to keep your posture in check, reduce the risk of injury, and avoid a decline in your swimming performance. Adding hip and back strength exercises to your dry-land training routine is highly recommended. Sample exercises include uphill running, bear crawls (walking like a bear on all fours), bench step-ups, squats, squat jumps, deadlifts, and core work. Participation in other sports such as soccer, basketball, and running can also help to strengthen the essential postural muscles of the hips and spine.

TEST SETS

Olympic swimmers are frequently tested to measure their current state of physical fitness, and what (if anything) needs to be added to their training regime to advance their swimming performance. It would be wise for you to do the same, so that you'll know if your body is up to the challenge and compatible with your current thinking and goals. The four do-it-yourself fitness tests that appear below are from world-renowned swimming researcher Dr. Brent Rushall, Professor Emeritus, at San Diego State University.

FRONT ABDOMINAL HOLD TEST

Introduction: This test is designed to measure the muscular strength and endurance of your frontal abdominal muscles. These muscles are essential for stabilizing your body in the water.

Expectation: Your challenge is to hold the test position (as outlined) for four minutes without change, but don't panic, because you can always start with one minute and work up from there.

Test Position: Lie face up on a comfortable flat surface. Next, bend your knees and draw your feet in toward your butt until your knees achieve a 90-degree bend with your feet flat on the ground. Next, raise your fully extended arms (with palms facing downwards) over your legs. Next, place your wrists forward of your knees with your fingers stretched. Do not rest your arms on your knees. At this point, your body should be in a half sit-up position with your entire back straight and off the ground. Once in position begin the test.

Caution: You must hold the test position precisely as outlined. Your arms must not bend, your wrist must remain forward of your knees, with your fingers stretched. It's critically important that you keep your arms in the test position as most swimming actions require an extended arm position.

Results: Holding the test position for four minutes straight suggests that you have sufficient muscular strength and endurance to maintain an adequate body position in any swimming event. With each repeated test, the quality of your performance should improve. If you experience a lack of improvement, you should add sit-ups, v-sits, and kip-ups to your dry-land training routine.

LUMBAR HOLD TEST

Introduction: This test is designed to measure the muscular strength and endurance of your lumbar region (lower back). These muscles are essential for stabilizing your body in the water.

Expectation: Your challenge is to hold the test position (as outlined) for four minutes without change, but don't panic, because you can always start with one minute and work up from there.

Test Position: Lie face down on a comfortable flat surface. Next, extend your arms fully forward of your shoulders with your fingers stretched. Next, fully extend your legs, with your feet together, and toes pointed. Your face should face directly downward with your nose gently touching the ground. Next, raise your fully extended arms (shoulder-width apart) and legs off the ground until your armpits and mid-thighs are no longer in contact with the ground. Once in position, begin the test.

Caution: You must hold the test position precisely as outlined. Your arms and legs must remain fully extended at all times, your fingers stretched, and your toes pointed. Also, your mid-thighs must remain off the ground.

Result: Holding the test position for four minutes straight suggests that you have sufficient muscular strength and endurance to maintain an adequate body position in any swimming event. With each repeated test, the quality of your performance should improve. If you experience a lack of improvement, you should add leg lifts and Swan Push-Ups (see YouTube) to your dry-land training routine.

HORIZONTAL ARM HOLD TEST

Introduction: The test is designed to measure the muscular strength and endurance of your forearms, wrists, and fingers that hold your arms and hands in position when swimming. Your ability to maintain the proper position is important for force production (pulling strength).

Expectation: Your challenge is to hold the test position (as outlined) for four minutes without change, but don't panic, because you can always start with one minute and work up from there.

Test Position: In this test, you're required to hold a dumbbell in the palm of each hand, but do not curl your fingers around them. The dumbbell weight should equal five percent of your total body weight. For example, if your weight is one hundred pounds, your selected weight should be five pounds. Next, sit in a chair holding the dumbbells in your hands. Your feet should be hip-width apart and planted firmly on the ground. Next, lean forward in the chair with your upper arms supported by your knees and your lower arms and hands ahead of your knees (with no support). Once in position, begin the test.

Caution: You must hold the test position precisely as outlined. Your arms must not shift from the original starting position. Also, your wrist cannot bend at any point nor can your fingers curl around the dumbbells. You must stop the test if any change occurs in either arm.

Result: Holding the test position for four minutes straight suggests that you have sufficient muscular strength and endurance to hold an adequate "arm-hand position" in any swimming event. With each repeated test, the quality of your performance should improve. If you experience a lack of improvement, you should add tennis ball squeezes, wrist curls, and forearm curls to your dry-land training routine.

STANDING LONG JUMP TEST

Introduction: The amount of power that you can generate through your legs is a good indicator of your overall leg fitness (leg endurance is another factor). The Standing Long Jump Test is a great way to measure leg power and relates very well to the starting and turning actions found in swimming.

Expectation: Your challenge is to perform five standing long jumps. Your score will be the average of your best three attempts.

Test Position: Stand with your feet aligned and hip-width apart (like your standing on a starting block). It's advisable to wear proper footwear for jumping. Next, bend forward and place your fingers on your toes. The position should look similar to a swimming racing start off the block. Next, spring forward from the starting position. No backswing of the arms is permitted. Upon landing, measure your distance from the start position to the finish position (where your feet land). Perform five trials and calculate the average of your best three attempts.

Results: A minimally acceptable distance is one that exceeds your height, so if you're five feet tall, your jump average should be five feet or more. With each repeated test, the quality of your performance should improve. If you experience a lack of improvement, you should add plyometric depth jumps, bounding (exaggerated strides with an emphasis on springing off the ground), and jump squats to your dry-land training routine.

BODY IMAGE

While I'm somewhat shy to admit it, when I was a teenage swimmer, I spent a fair amount of time looking at myself in the mirror. If I looked in "swimming shape" it sent my confidence sky-high, and if not, it created doubt in my mind. I believe the same thing happens to any swimmer who gazes into the mirror. If their body looks super-fit, their confidence skyrockets, and if not, they experience an attack of self-doubt. To keep your swimming journey on track, I suggest that you look into the mirror at least once a week. If you like what you see, stay on course, and if not, it's time to eat smarter and work harder so that you have a body you're proud of.

SPORTS NUTRITION QUIZ

Talk, talk, talk, I talk a lot about the importance of nutrition and the positive impact it has on athletic performance. Unfortunately, some swimmers refuse to listen and prefer to follow the "See Food Diet" instead. In other words, whatever food they SEE, they eat! That may include brownies and pop tarts for breakfast and spare ribs, pizza, and a hot fudge sundae for dinner! A steady diet of these foods will no doubt cause swimmers to stink up the pool in more ways than one! Hopefully, you're not a disciple of this diet plan and have a solid understanding of the how, what, and when of sports nutrition. To test your knowledge take this quiz:

1. Swimmers need the same foods as less active people, only more of it.
   - ☐ True
   - ☐ False
   - ☐ Don't Know

2. The training diet for swimmers should be about 60% carbohydrate, 15-20% protein, and 20-30% fat.
   - ☐ True
   - ☐ False
   - ☐ Don't Know

3. Protein is the primary fuel for muscles.
   - ☐ True
   - ☐ False
   - ☐ Don't Know

4. A low-fat diet is necessary for losing body fat.
   - ☐ True

☐ False
☐ Don't Know

5. Whole wheat pita bread, bananas, fortified breakfast cereals, rice, corn, chocolate milk, pasta, orange juice, and potatoes are all carbohydrate-rich foods.
☐ True
☐ False
☐ Don't Know

6. Swimmers can build muscle by eating a well-balanced diet (with sufficient calories) and engaging in intense training both in and out of the pool.
☐ True
☐ False
☐ Don't Know

7. Before practice, it's important to eat protein.
☐ True
☐ False
☐ Don't Know

8. After practice, it's essential to have more protein than carbohydrates.
☐ True
☐ False
☐ Don't Know

9. The process of losing excess body fat should begin well before the most competitive part of the season or year.
☐ True

☐ False
☐ Don't Know

10. Of the following three choices, which one is the best pre-competition meal?

☐ Hot dog, fries, and coleslaw.

☐ Pasta served with tomato sauce.

☐ Pasta served with meat sauce, a small side salad, and fruit.

11. Ideally, the pre-competition meal should be consumed two to three hours before competition.

☐ True

☐ False

☐ Don't Know

12. A sports drink would be the best choice for competition because (choose any that apply).

☐ It has half the sugar of fruit juice or soda.

☐ It helps to keep blood sugar from dropping through the day.

☐ It contains electrolytes (salts that are a natural part of your bodily fluids).

☐ All are true.

13. Refueling the body within 15-30 minutes after intense training is highly recommended.

☐ True

☐ False

☐ Don't Know

14. The primary muscle fuel for intense training, competition, and recovery after exercise is (select one).

☐ Protein

☐ Carbohydrate

☐ Fat

15. Smart recovery foods choices include (select the one incorrect answer).

☐ Chocolate milk and a banana
☐ Isolated whey protein powder
☐ Sports drink and an energy bar

Note: *You will find answers to the Sports Nutrition Quiz on the following pages. Turn the book up-side-down to see the correct responses.*

SPORTS NUTRITION QUIZ ANSWERS

juice, sports drinks, crackers) which are fast release and sources of quick energy. After that, they should follow up with a well-balanced meal consisting of carbohydrates, protein, and fat.

9. Answer: True

Why? The start of the swim season is usually less physically intense requiring fewer calories per day. During the most competitive time, swimmers should consume as many smart calories as possible to keep up with the demanding workloads.

10. Answer: Pasta served with meat sauce, a small side salad, and fruit.

Why? This meal is a good source of carbohydrates and contains a moderate amount of protein and fat.

11. Answer: True

Why? This allows time for adequate digestion and enables the fuel to reach the muscles in time.

12. Answer: All are true

Why? Sports drinks are specially formulated to enter the bloodstream quickly so that water and carbohydrates get to the working muscles as fast as possible.

13. Answer: True

Why? Immediately after training, swimmers should eat a snack containing carbohydrates along with a small amount of protein. A few crackers with cheese, yogurt, or a handful of dried fruits and nuts will suffice.

14. Answer: Carbohydrate

Why? Carbohydrates are the highest source of energy. Proteins supply the muscles with less than five percent.

15. Answer: Isolated whey protein powder

Why? Isolated whey protein powder is not an adequate recovery fuel. Chocolate milk and a banana or a sports drink and an energy bar are excellent sources of carbohydrates and help to refuel the muscles immediately after training or competition.

1. Answer: True

Why? Swimmers who train intensely need more servings of each food group than others.

2. Answer: True

Why? Carbohydrates are vital to maintaining energy balance, fueling working muscles, and energizing the brain. Protein is essential for growing and repairing tissue. Fat is a crucial carrier of fat-soluble vitamins and supplies essential fatty acids.

3. Answer: False

Why? Carbohydrates are the primary muscle fuel. Insufficient amounts can cause the muscles to break down and waste away.

4. Answer: False

Why? Eating a well-balanced diet and expending more calories per day (than consumed) leads to weight loss.

5. Answer: True

Why? Grain products (bread, cereal, crackers, pasta, rice), fruits, some vegetables, and milk products all provide carbohydrates for energy.

6. Answer: True

Why? Smart eating plus hard work creates the body of a champion.

7. Answer: False

Why? It's important to eat foods high in carbohydrates (before practice or competition), together with a moderate amount of protein and fat. A small amount of protein and fat help to regulate the rate of energy release from foods high in carbohydrates.

8. Answer: False

Why? Immediately after training, swimmers should restore their glycogen stores with simple carbohydrates (fruit

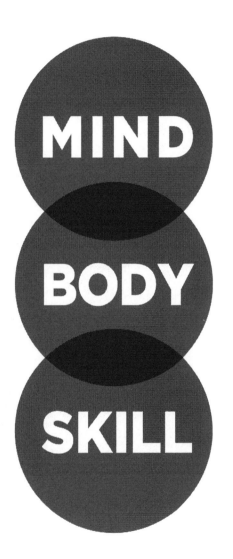

SKILL WORK

INTRODUCTION

When racing, do you rely primarily on your physical assets for speed, your technical assets, or both? If you're like most swimmers, it's physical. While training without an emphasis on technique can work in the short term, it can't deliver the speed needed to compete at the highest levels, because swimmers at the top have spent years integrating their technical skills with their physical ones. Swimmers often tell me that when they focus on their technique in practice, they go slower and can't keep up the pace. While this may be true in the short-run, in the long run strokes that are superior in both skill and fitness rule the pool! If you don't believe me, go online and watch the swimming finals from the Beijing, London, or Rio Olympics. What you'll find is that every Olympic finalist has top-notch technique and they got that way by training technically smart and physically hard every day in practice.

BE A ROCK ON THE BLOCK

Have you ever heard of the sensational runner Usain Bolt? If you haven't, you must be living on another planet! He's considered the greatest sprinter of all time, winning nine Olympic gold medals, and also the world record holder in the 100 and 200 meters. If you observe him on video, you'll notice that his track start is very similar to the one used in swimming, and in fact, runners used the track start well before swimmers did. I've watched numerous videos of Usain racing on YouTube, and noticed how his muscles tighten (contract) before he blasts off the block. Do your muscles do that? Chances are they don't, but if they did, you'd have a stronger, straighter, and faster start because tensing your muscles puts them on high alert and ready for immediate action. To master this essential skill, all you have to do is make your entire body feel like a "rock on the block" before blasting off. On a side note, this technique also applies to the backstroke start.

BODY BALANCE

I love watching the MLB World Series (major league baseball). One thing that amazes me is how fast a pitcher can throw the ball and how far a batter can hit it. But it's more than strength that contributes to the distance; it's also balance. In other words, the players know how to balance their bodies (before pitching or swinging) so that they can generate maximum force. Take a look at the amount of time a pitcher takes to prepare before throwing or the amount of time a batter takes to prepare before swinging, and you'll see what I mean.

Balance also plays a significant role in swimming. For example, a swimmer cannot exert the maximum force (in any stroke) if their body isn't in a balanced state first. To avoid this performance pitfall, I strongly recommend that you give these technical tips a try. In the butterfly, make sure that you execute a full chest-press action before initiating the pull. In the backstroke and freestyle, your hand, hip, and foot must assume a straight and balanced line before the pull begins. And in the breaststroke, make sure that the back of your hands, the back of your head, and the soles of your feet are in a straight line before initiating the sweep-out phase of the pull.

5-POINT BREASTSTROKE KICK

I recently read an article about Rebecca Soni, one of the greatest female breaststrokers of all time. Her amazing achievements speak for themselves, breaking six world records in the 100 and 200 breaststrokes combined. She's also the first woman to go under 2:20:00 in the 200-breaststroke

(LCM). What's the secret to her phenomenal success? There are too many to list, but one of her stellar attributes was her ability to generate 100 "thrust pounds" of force per kick (versus 20 thrust pounds per pull). To achieve a number like that, she needed super-strong legs plus Olympic-level skill. To upgrade your breaststroke kick give these five ideas a try:

1. Don't bend your knees on the leg recovery. Draw your heels up to your butt instead as it will help to reduce thigh drag.

2. Keep your feet and knees inside your shoulder width as you draw your heels to your butt.

3. Rotate your feet outward, as far as possible, before kicking back as it will allow your feet to "grab" the most amount of water.

4. Snap the finish of your kick. In other words, to generate the most amount of thrust from your legs and feet, the finish phase of the kick cycle must be twice as fast as the start phase.

5. Point your toes backward (not downward) at the completion of your kick to reduce the amount of foot drag.

CHIN UP BACKSTROKE

Sometimes the smallest things can make the most significant difference. The simple act of pointing your chin upward toward the sky (versus downward toward your chest) when swimming backstroke can help to raise your hips, legs, and feet closer to the surface and reduce drag. It also makes it easier for your body to rotate from side-to-side because a straight body turns better than a curved one.

11-ARMS BUTTERFLY

I love watching Michael Phelps swim butterfly, and I liken him to a swimming genius. In my mind, his stroke is as perfect as humanly possible, and I could go on all day singing his praises. One thing that stands out in particular is his "11-Arms" at the beginning and end of each pull cycle. In other words, his arms look like the number "11" when they enter and exit the water. To have arms like that at the entry point, you must place them into the water fully extended and directly forward of your shoulders. To have arms like that at the finish point, you must follow through with your pull until your arms are fully extended and flush to the sides of your body. Finishing with a full pull is extremely challenging as it requires a great deal of upper body strength.

POP YOUR PULL OUT

Ideally, swimmers should explode through the surface off a breaststroke pull out, but unfortunately, most float to the surface instead. The problem is typically caused by going too deep off the start (or turn) or holding each phase of the pull out for too long, creating a loss of momentum. As a result, swimmers either come up to the surface on a steep incline or surface with zero speed. To avoid this speed-reducing problem, I created a breaststroke turning concept known as the "5 Pops." In this case, pop refers to an action that's explosive.

Pop 1: Pop off the wall, don't push off the wall.
Pop 2: Pop your dolphin kick, either before or after you pull down.
Pop 3: Pop the bottom of your pull down.
Pop 4: Pop your streamlined arms as you rise to the surface.
Pop 5: Pop your first stroke when you break the surface.

By combining all 5 Pops into your breaststroke pull-out sequence, you'll come out way ahead of the competition!

FREESTYLE NOSE NUMBER

Keeping the chin up in backstroke can do wonders for the stroke. Keeping the nose down in freestyle can have the same effect. Due to improper teaching, a lack of focus, or crowded pools, I find that most swimmers swim freestyle with their heads too high causing a multitude of problems including a loss of stability, a broken body line or kick, reduced side-to-side rotation, and increased drag. To rectify this problem and to establish the proper head position, I recommend the Nose Number Drill as follows:

1. Start by kicking freestyle down the pool with your arms forward of your shoulders (shoulder-width apart) and your nose pointing directly downward toward the bottom of the pool. This is known as "1 Nose Number."

2. Continue to travel down the pool, but slowly tilt your nose upward to "2 Nose Number," then 3, then 4, then 5. On "5 Nose Number," your mouth should break the surface allowing for a breath. Repeat the same process over and over again until you reach the other end of the pool.

3. Swim freestyle using the same method. By the end, you'll notice that a "1 or 2 Nose Number" works best and makes your freestyle feel better and faster.

HEAD LIFT VERSUS SHOULDER RISE

Lifting the head to breathe in the butterfly and breaststroke is a definite no-no, yet it's a common practice in swimming. The correct method of breathing is not the result of a head-lift action, but rather, a shoulder-rise action that occurs at a specific point in both the butterfly and breaststroke pull.

In the butterfly, it's when the pulling arms pass underneath the shoulder/chest area, and in the breast-stroke, it's when the sculling arms move inside shoulder width. You'd be very wise to wait for the breath and allow your arms to raise your body upwards to the point where you can breathe naturally and without force.

BREAKOUT ANGLE

Take a piece of paper and draw a five-degree angle on it. Now imagine breaking out at that same angle in your starts and turns. Sound weird? Not so, because that's the way Olympians do it. An angle more substantial than that increases frontal drag and interrupts the desired flow between the underwater portion of a start or turn and the breakout. Achieving the desired angle on a front or back start can be tricky especially if you enter the water on a steep incline. To rectify the problem, point your streamlined arms and head (combined) immediately upward to redirect your body to the surface. Turns are much easier to adjust because typically you're not as deep (compared to a start). All you have to do is point your arms toward the other end of the pool rather than down to the bottom when you push off the wall. A five-degree breakout angle is guaranteed to speed up your starts and turns.

STROKE TIMING

Start a stopwatch and watch the seconds tick away. As you watch, imagine swimming backstroke or freestyle to that timing with your right arm entering the water on one, your left arm entering the water on two, and so on. I call it "one-second timing" and you can use it to set your stroke rhythm for the 100 backstroke and 100 freestyle. For 50s (in both strokes), aim for a time slightly faster than one second, and 200s (in both strokes), strive for a time slightly slower than one second. Focus on all three timings in practice while maintaining the most extended stroke possible. Continue week-to-week until each becomes second nature to you. On a side note, Olympians achieve numbers (in the backstroke and freestyle) that are closer to 00.50 seconds in the 50s, 00.60 seconds in the 100s, and 00.70 seconds in the 200s! Perhaps you'll hit those numbers one day in the future.

SHOULDER-HIP ROTATION

As mentioned previously, 29 different muscle groups make up the core. To ensure that you engage as many of them as possible when swimming the backstroke and freestyle, I recommend rotating your shoulders and hips together versus only your shoulders or only your hips. To do that, imagine steel bars connecting your shoulders to your hips as you turn from side-to-side. Swimmers who incorporate this concept into their swimming, experience a fuller rotation and a much stronger pull.

ADD MORE ZIP TO YOUR FLIP

There are two forward flip turns in swimming, one for the backstroke and the other for the freestyle. On the backstroke flip turn, you perform a forward somersault on your stomach, land flat on your back, and push off on your back. On the freestyle flip turn, you execute a forward somersault on your stomach, land flat on your back, push off on your back, twist to your side first, and to your stomach second. The breakout portion of the backstroke turn is much easier to execute because you stay on your back the entire time, but the breakout portion of the freestyle turn is much trickier because you must twist your entire body 180 degrees (from back to front) before surfacing. To avoid getting stuck on your side when coming off the wall, I recommend twisting entirely onto your stomach by the time your feet depart the wall. It's much easier to do, and it places you in the ideal position for freestyle.

GYMNAST OFF THE BLOCK

With a little amount of training, Olympic gymnastic sensation Simone Biles would crush any swimmer on a backstroke start because she's super-flexible and dramatically explosive. Due to her physical attributes, she'd achieve an immediate "bridge position" off the block as well a tight streamlining of the arms behind her head. The majority of swimmers (that I encounter) have a tough time getting into a full-bridge position and manage to get their arms only partially behind their heads before entering the water. The most efficient way to improve your bridging action is to practice Bridges on the pool deck, in dry-land, or at home. Performing Overhead Med Ball Throws is a great way to accelerate the throwing action of your arms. A daily stretch of your Pectoralis Major and Terres Major muscle groups will open up your chest area making it easier for you to throw your arms fully overhead. If you're unfamiliar with Bridges or Overhead Med Ball Throws, I suggest searching both on YouTube.

FAST HANDS, FAST HEAD

The breaststroke pull consists of three phases including the sweep, the scull, and the shoot. The pull builds in speed from beginning to end with the shoot being the fastest phase of all. At the peak of the scull, the head rises for the breath (via the torso), and from there, it lunges aggressively forward. Maximizing momentum and flow (at this point in the stroke) is key to a fast breaststroke, so the head must move forward at the speed of the hands and assume a "submarine position" (body entirely underwater) at the point of maximum streamline.

15-YEAR-OLD 10 & UNDER SWIMMERS

Most 10 & Under swimmers swim like wind-up toys. They spin their wheels, bounce up and down like basketballs, and squirm like worms. In their minds, stroke rate, regardless of stroke efficiency, is the only way to go. Surprisingly, I see a lot of 15-year-old swimmers (and swimmers of other ages for that matter) embrace the same approach! In the last year, how many new skills have you added to your "swimming toolbox?" As you grow in age, you must also increase your level of technical sophistication. If not, you'll find it increasingly difficult to stay up with the pack.

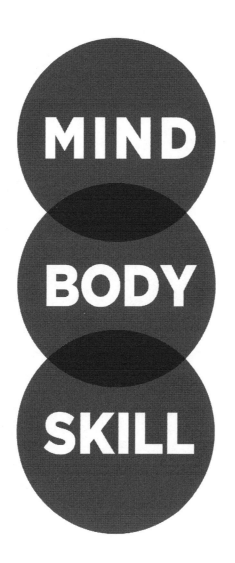

THE LAST WORD

So you've finally reached the end of my book, congratulations! I hope and pray that you felt it was a worthwhile read and that you walk away with some fresh insights on how to catapult your swimming to the next level. Promise me that you'll never stand still and that you'll pursue improvement with passion and zest. If you ever have the opportunity, I would love to meet you in person at one of my many swim camps and clinics. Until then, I wish you much success along your journey!

41345008R00033

Made in the USA
Columbia, SC
15 December 2018